SACRAMENTO PUBLIC LIBRARY
828 "I" Street
Sacramento, CA   95814
6/10

D0772782

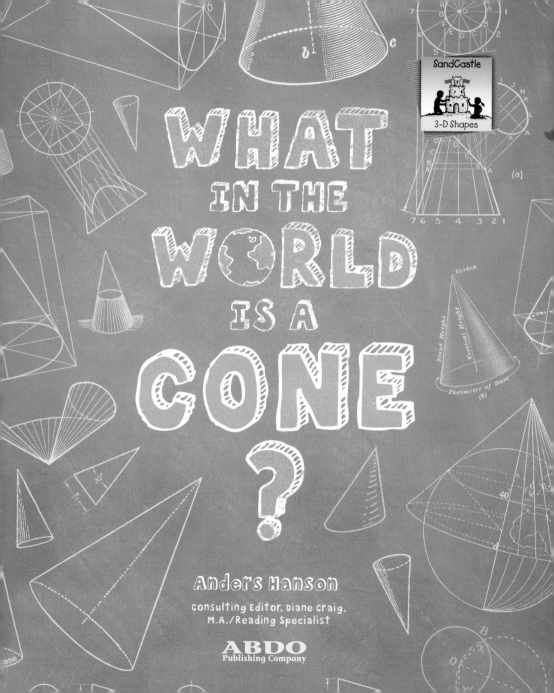

SandCastle
3-D Shapes

WHAT
IN THE
WORLD
IS A
CONE
?

Anders Hanson

consulting Editor, Diane craig,
M.A./Reading Specialist

ABDO
Publishing Company

Published by ABDO Publishing Company, 8000 West 78th Street, Edina, MN 55439.

Copyright © 2008 by Abdo Consulting Group, Inc. International copyrights reserved in all countries.

No part of this book may be reproduced in any form without written permission from the publisher. SandCastle™ is a trademark and logo of ABDO Publishing Company.

Printed in the United States.
Editor: Pam Price
Curriculum Coordinator: Nancy Tuminelly
Cover and Interior Design and Production: Mighty Media
Photo Credits: JupiterImages Corporation, ShutterStock

Library of Congress Cataloging-in-Publication Data

Hanson, Anders, 1980-
   What in the world is a cone? / Anders Hanson.
      p. cm. -- (3-D shapes)
   ISBN-13: 978-1-59928-886-4
   1. Cone--Juvenile literature. 2. Shapes--Juvenile literature. 3. Geometry, Solid--Juvenile literature.
I. Title.
   QA491.H357 2008
   516'.154--dc22

                          2007015629

SandCastle™ Level: Transitional

| **Emerging Readers** | **Beginning Readers** | **Transitional Readers** | **Fluent Readers** |
| (no flags) | (1 flag) | (2 flags) | (3 flags) |

SandCastle™ would like to hear from you. Please send us your comments or questions.

sandcastle@abdopublishing.com

SandCastle™ books are created by a team of professional educators, reading specialists, and content developers around five essential components—phonemic awareness, phonics, vocabulary, text comprehension, and fluency—to assist young readers as they develop reading skills and strategies and increase their general knowledge. All books are written, reviewed, and leveled for guided reading, early reading intervention, and Accelerated Reader® programs for use in shared, guided, and independent reading and writing activities to support a balanced approach to literacy instruction. The SandCastle™ series has four levels that correspond to early literacy development. The levels are provided to help teachers and parents select appropriate books for young readers.

3-D shapes are all around us.

3-D stands for 3-dimensional.

It means that an object is not flat.

A cone is a 3-D shape.

APEX

BASE

A cone has an apex and a round base.

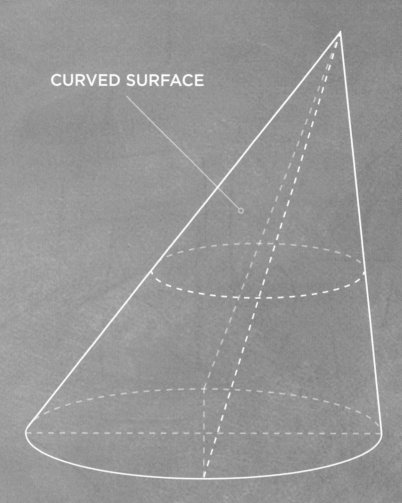

CURVED SURFACE

The apex and the base are joined by a curved surface.

Cones are everywhere!

James loves to
eat ice cream.

He likes it best
when it comes
in a cone.

Today is Sally's birthday!

Her birthday hat is shaped like a cone.

The tipis used by
American Indians
of the Great Plains
are cone shaped.

Cones often form
when fine material
is poured into a pile.

Cones are
sometimes
built on top
of towers.

16

Traffic cones
alert drivers
to obstacles
or detours.

A wind sock
shows which
direction the
wind is blowing.

This wind sock
is cone shaped.

19

Find the cone!

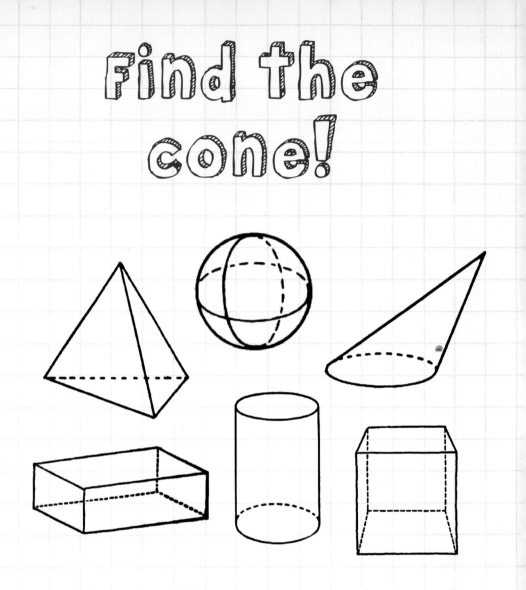

Which one of these 3-D shapes is a cone?

How many cones can you find in this photo?

21

Everyday cones

Take a look around you.

Do you see any cones?

How to draw a cone

1. Draw a curve.

2. Draw a point above the curve.

3. Connect the endpoints of the curve to the point.

Glossary

apex – the highest point.

curve – to bend smoothly without any sharp angles.

detour – a temporary route taken instead of the main road.

dimensional – having a measurement of length, width, or thickness.

endpoint – a point at the end of a line segment or a ray.

obstacle – something that blocks progress.

To see a complete list of SandCastle™ books and other nonfiction titles from ABDO Publishing Company, visit www.abdopublishing.com.
8000 West 78th Street, Edina, MN 55439 · 800-800-1312 · 952-831-1632 fax